D0849484

EXTREME CAREERS™

SEARCH-AND-RESCUE SWIMMERS

Laura La Bella

rosen publishing's
rosen
central®

New York

Published in 2009 by The Rosen Publishing Group, Inc.
29 East 21st Street, New York, NY 10010

Copyright © 2009 by The Rosen Publishing Group, Inc.

First Edition

Library of Congress Cataloging-in-Publication Data

La Bella, Laura.
Search and rescue swimmers / Laura La Bella.—1st ed.
    p. cm.—(Extreme careers)
ISBN-13: 978-1-4042-1786-7 (library binding)
1. Lifesaving—Juvenile literature. 2. Search and rescue operations—Juvenile literature. 3. Lifesaving—Vocational guidance—Juvenile literature. 4. Search and rescue operations—Vocational guidance—Juvenile literature. I. Title.
VK1445.L3 2007
797.2'00289—dc22

                                                    2007047306

Manufactured in Malaysia

On the cover: A Coast Guard rescue helicopter hoists Guard officers Rob Updike and Mike Heximer from the Gulf of Mexico in a demonstration in St. Petersburg, Florida.

Contents

Introduction

When you face an emergency in your home, you immediately call 9-1-1 for help. But what happens when you are in a boat, out at sea? There is no 9-1-1 to call. So what do you do? Out at sea, the job of emergency rescue falls to the United States Coast Guard, a branch of the military that operates under the Department of Homeland Security.

According to its Web site, every day, the U.S. Coast Guard saves 15 lives, assists 114 people in distress, and conducts 82 search-and-rescue missions around the world. Search-and-rescue swimmers are the men and women on the front lines when a distress call comes to report a person—civilian or military—on the high seas who needs to be rescued. Nearly every rescue requires the search-and-rescue swimmer to put his or her own life in danger to save a stranger.

Among the most highly trained in the military forces, search-and-rescue swimmers can be trained through the U.S. Coast Guard, Navy, Marine Corps, or Air Force. Each of these military forces has a training program for search-and-rescue swimmers.

Programs range from five weeks (to learn basic skills) to more than two years (for intensive search-and-rescue training). The more extensive programs, offered by the U.S. Coast Guard and U.S. Air Force, prepare their search-and-rescue swimmers for almost every imaginable scenario they could face during a rescue. Their training is so intensive and challenging that nearly half of all candidates drop out.

Search-and-rescue swimmers are among the best of the best in the armed forces. They are on call twenty-four hours a day at more than twenty-eight air stations across the United States. They are deployed within minutes of receiving a distress call. Their job of protecting and rescuing is not without its risks. Faced with the coldest and stormiest of waters, they must dive in where others would quickly drown. These men and women have the swimming skill and athletic ability of Olympians, and it is not unusual for rescues to take anywhere from twelve to fifteen hours, depending on the situation. It is an extreme career, one full of challenges and rewards.

Hurricane Katrina

At 7:00 AM on August 29, 2005, Hurricane Katrina made landfall on the Louisiana coast between Grand Isle and the mouth of the Mississippi River. The governor of Louisiana, Kathleen Blanco, ordered the complete evacuation of the city of New Orleans and its surrounding areas. But even though mandatory evacuation warnings had been issued for several days for the category 4 storm, thousands of residents stayed in their homes. They either would not or could not leave their homes and thus stayed to face one of the strongest storms in the history of the United States.

The fierce storm, the sixth strongest Atlantic hurricane ever recorded and the third strongest hurricane on record to make landfall in the United States, caused massive devastation. The most severe loss of life and property occurred in the city of New Orleans. In the hours immediately after the storm, the city continued to experience massive flooding as the levee system broke under the pressure of the storm's wind and rain. More than 80 percent of the city was flooded. Thousands of people

Residents of an apartment building in New Orleans flooded by Hurricane Katrina signal for help. The hurricane left more than 80 percent of the city of New Orleans underwater.

were stranded. Some, to escape the rising floodwaters that overtook their homes and neighborhoods, found temporary safety in their attics and on their roofs. Some floated on debris in the actual floodwaters. All of them awaited rescue.

On Standby

In the days before the hurricane made landfall, as the country watched the storm gain strength, pass over islands in the Caribbean Sea, and cause damage in the lower panhandle of

Florida, a quiet mobilization was occurring. On August 26, in preparation for the storm, the Coast Guard began prepositioning rescue teams and resources. It activated more than four hundred reservists, closed ports and waterways along the Gulf Coast, and evacuated its own personnel and equipment from air stations in the path of the hurricane. More than forty Coast Guard seacraft from units along the entire eastern seaboard—including more than thirty small boats, patrol boats, and cutters—were positioned around the area. All of them were ready to conduct post-hurricane search-and-rescue operations as soon as the weather calmed enough to make deployment safe.

Search-and-rescue crews were monitoring the storm at air stations in Cape Cod, Massachusetts; Clearwater, Florida; Atlantic City, New Jersey; Elizabeth City, North Carolina; Savannah, Georgia; and Mobile, Alabama. Rescue crews were placed on standby. As they waited for the storm to pass, they monitored the weather, discussed the various rescue scenarios they might face, and checked and rechecked their equipment. The crews knew that as soon as they were given the go-ahead, they would board helicopters and fly into the hardest-hit areas in search of survivors. Little did they know they were preparing for one of the largest search-and-rescue operations in the history of the United States.

The first rescues occurred when aircraft and rescue swimmers were dispatched to save boaters and fishermen who were at sea as the hurricane passed over them. Once the hurricane passed over New Orleans and began to travel inland, search-and-rescue

A Coast Guard helicopter deploys a search-and-rescue swimmer to save a stranded New Orleans resident. More than 33,545 people were rescued in the New Orleans area.

The *Mary Lynn* Encounters Hurricane Katrina

On August 29 and 30, as Hurricane Katrina churned in the Gulf of Mexico, the fishing boat *Mary Lynn*, with a crew of two men and one woman, began taking on water. At about 8:00 PM, the crew sounded an emergency beacon as the hurricane beat down on them. At about 9:00 PM, a rescue helicopter took off from Clearwater, Florida. Coast Guard lieutenant Craig Massello, commander of a Jayhawk helicopter, and his crew took a direct route to the boat, flying straight into the hurricane—a dangerous thing to do. The hurricane's fierce eighty-five-knot winds were blowing the helicopter off course and using up more fuel than a normal flight. By the time the crew reached the *Mary Lynn* at 1:30 AM, it was completely dark. And by now, Hurricane Katrina was raging. Even using night-vision goggles, the pilots could barely see the *Mary Lynn* and its crew. Fearing the helicopter's struggle against the severe winds would use up their remaining fuel, the pilots made the tough decision to leave the boat behind and fly to a naval air station in Key West, Florida, to refuel.

They returned to the *Mary Lynn* at 5:30 AM It was still dark. Each time they approached the boat, the intense winds kept blowing the helicopter away. After several tries, the pilots decided it would be safer to hover nearby until daylight, hoping the hurricane's winds would calm enough so they could attempt to rescue the *Mary Lynn*'s crew. At around 7:30, the Coast Guard crew moved back into position. Looking down at the boat, Lieutenant Massello could see waves rising about forty-five feet high (about fourteen meters). Petty Officer Kenyon Bolton, a rescue swimmer, was lowered into the sea by a hoist with assistance from Petty Officer Rob Cain, the flight mechanic. One by one, the *Mary Lynn*'s crewmembers got into a flotation ring that was attached to their fishing boat. They fought the high winds and waves to swim out toward Bolton, who guided them. As each one made his or her way to him, Bolton strapped the crewmembers into the rescue basket and Cain raised them using the hoist. The Coast Guard crew was able to save all three of the Mary Lynn's crewmembers and get them to safety.

The Coast Guard crew who made the daring rescue of the *Mary Lynn*.

personnel began flying over neighborhoods to look for survivors. Many rescue teams immediately spotted people on rooftops. For nearly all of the search-and-rescue teams, this was a very different experience than what they had trained for. Search-and-rescue swimmers were used to dropping into the ocean from helicopters to rescue sailors or civilians whose ships had capsized. Many were now dropping into floodwaters in residential areas where there were homes and much dangerous debris under the water. These were dangerous conditions for rescuers, and in response to this new challenge, urban search-and-rescue techniques were developed on the fly. In addition, few aircrews had experience flying night missions through a flooded city where high winds and live, hanging power lines added to the danger. For the search-and-rescue crews, this was a completely new experience that put their training to the test.

A Record Number of Rescues

After the Hurricane Katrina rescue missions ended, it was reported that more than 33,545 people had been rescued. Of these, 12,533 lives were saved by air resources, and 11,584 lives were saved by surface resources. The Coast Guard had single-handedly rescued more than 24,000 people and assisted with the joint-agency evacuation of some 9,000 others. More than 9,403 patients were evacuated from hospitals and brought to safer ground. At the height of rescue operations, the Coast Guard had 62 aircraft, 30 cutters, and 111 small boats assisting in rescue and recovery operations. Approximately one-third of the Coast Guard's entire air fleet was deployed to the New Orleans region to support rescue operations in the immediate aftermath of the hurricane. More than 5,290 Coast Guard personnel conducted search-and-rescue operations, waterway reconstitution, and environmental assessment operations. More than 400 Coast Guard reservists were recalled to active duty.

How It Began

Search-and-rescue swimmers, as we know them now, were unheard of until the 1980s. One major maritime disaster changed all that when a marine vessel, the *Marine Electric*, capsized in a large storm in the Atlantic Ocean off the coast of Virginia. At the time, the Coast Guard was not prepared, nor did it have the manpower, to respond to a distress call of such magnitude. The incident led to a congressional mandate that gave the Coast Guard the authority to create a rescue swimmer program and staff its air stations throughout the United States with search-and-rescue swimmers.

The *Marine Electric*

On February 12, 1983, the *Marine Electric* departed from Norfolk, Virginia, loaded with 27,000 tons of coal. Under the command of Captain Philip Corl, the ship was en route to the New England Power Plant at Brayton Point, Massachusetts.

The S.S. *Marine Electric* rests at the Bethlehem Steel Company's Boston yard. The ship was involved in an accident that led to a major overhaul in Coast Guard operations and influenced the establishment of the search-and-rescue swimmer program.

The ship was fighting through a heavy storm in the Atlantic Ocean when the Coast Guard asked the vessel to turn around and aid a smaller ship, the *Theodora*, which had begun taking on water. The *Marine Electric* reached the *Theodora* just as the smaller vessel was navigating toward shelter. The Coast Guard asked the *Marine Electric* to shadow the smaller ship until it could make it to safety. Once the *Theodora* was safe, the *Marine Electric* turned north and resumed its original course.

The ship continued traveling north but made little progress as it battled against twenty-foot (six meters) waves. The bow of the ship began taking on water. As the crew scrambled to assist the captain, it became evident that the ship was going under. The crew was sent to begin preparing the lifeboats. They were swung out over the side of the vessel but not lowered. The ship was now listing, or tilting, to one side and taking on more water. Captain Corl radioed the Coast Guard to ask if there were any ships in the vicinity that could be sent to help them. The closest ship was two to three hours away. At the rate the ship was taking on water, the *Marine Electric* would sink before the boat got to them.

Having given the order to abandon ship, Captain Corl radioed the Coast Guard again and informed them. The crew rushed to board the lifeboats, but it was too late. The *Marine Electric* suddenly capsized and tossed nearly its whole crew into the water. As the waves crashed against them and as the wind and rain pounded the ocean, the crewmen struggled to reach the lifeboats. The pounding surf pulled crewmen away from the ship and into the darkness. Two crewmen fought to help the others, but it was useless. The storm was too powerful.

The Coast Guard Sends Help

The Coast Guard, responding to the captain's order to abandon ship, sent a rescue helicopter from Coast Guard Air Station Elizabeth City in North Carolina. By the time the aircraft was on the scene, the *Marine Electric* had sunk, and most of the thirty-four crewmen were fighting for their lives in the frigid waters of the Atlantic Ocean. Many had already begun to drown. As a helicopter hovered overhead, a rescue basket was prepared and lowered to the crewmembers in the water. The water was so cold that most of the crewmen were numb from severe hypothermia. They could not grab onto the rescue basket. Recognizing that these victims could not be rescued without additional help, the Coast Guard placed an immediate call to request a U.S. Navy helicopter and rescue swimmer. The navy scrambled up a crew and was on the scene quickly.

Aboard the navy helicopter was diver James D. McCann, who dove into the freezing waters in search of survivors. He swam to the point of exhaustion in 40-foot (12 m) seas in an effort to save as many crewmen as he could. Conditions were so severe and the temperatures so cold that the seawater on his facemask froze. In the freezing waters, as the hours passed, McCann could save only three crewmembers. Thirty-one crewmembers from the *Marine Electric* perished that night.

Tragedy Leads to Change

In the months after the *Marine Electric* sank, an investigation was launched into the incident. The House of Representatives' Merchant Marine and Fisheries Committee held hearings. It questioned why the world's premier maritime rescue service, the Coast Guard, was unable to directly assist people in the water. The investigation revealed that the existing techniques and

Rescue Swimmers in the Media

Search-and-rescue swimmers have been featured in a number of films. Two of the most popular are *The Guardian* and *Top Gun*. *The Guardian*, released in 2006, stars Kevin Costner as a legendary rescue swimmer and Ashton Kutcher as his young protégé. In *Top Gun*, Tom Cruise, a naval pilot, is rescued by a search-and-rescue swimmer when his plane crashes in the ocean, killing his copilot.

equipment were inadequate for rescues in extreme conditions, such as those that occurred during the *Marine Electric* rescue. As a result, Congress mandated in the Coast Guard Authorization Act of 1984 that "the Commandant of the Coast Guard shall . . . establish a helicopter rescue swimmer program for the purpose of training selected Coast Guard personnel in rescue swimming skills." With this mandate, Coast Guard Headquarters' Aviation Division turned its attention to developing and training rescue specialists who could assist incapacitated people in the water. An official search-and-rescue swimmer program was established.

As fate would have it, some sixteen years later, the Coast Guard would find itself facing a challenge similar to that of the *Marine Electric*. On a cold December day in 1999, during a major storm, the *Sea Breeze*, a marine vessel, radioed for help. Again, thirty-four lives were at stake in freezing weather conditions off the coast of North Carolina. Coast Guard Air Station

An HH-60 Jayhawk helicopter from Air Station Elizabeth City, North Carolina, responds to a distress call from the *Sea Breeze I*. The Coast Guard safely rescued the thirty-four-member crew from the vessel.

Elizabeth City again responded and went into action, but this time with fully trained rescue swimmers. The Coast Guard was able to save all thirty-four crewmen from the *Sea Breeze*, avoiding a repeat of the *Marine Electric* tragedy.

Experience Leads to More Training

As rescue swimmers were deployed into more and more situations, the need for additional training became evident. In

Regular training missions keep search-and-rescue swimmers' skills sharp. During this training session off the coast of Oahu, Hawaii, search-and-rescue swimmers from Air Station Barbers Point practice basket drills.

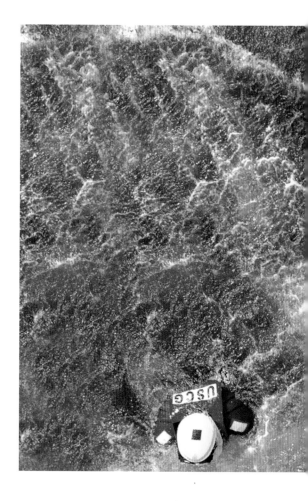

February 1991, another near tragedy led to the implementation of further training for this elite group of rescuers, when, in responding to the distress call of a stranded hiker, a rescue swimmer was nearly killed along Oregon's rugged coastline. The rescue swimmer, Petty Officer Patrick Chick, was responding to

a distress call made by a stranded hiker who was stuck on a
steep cliff above Lincoln Beach. Chick deployed from a rescue
helicopter onto the cliff to assist the hiker. As Chick tried to
get the hiker secured into the rescue basket, he lost his footing
and fell 120 feet (36.5 m) from the cliff to the beach below.

Luckily, he sustained only minor injuries, thanks to his training and the protective gear he was wearing.

The accident illustrated a flaw in deployment procedures, and after a review of the incident, new techniques were put into practice. Now, the rescue swimmer would remain attached to the hoist cable and be deployed directly to a survivor. This was safer for the rescuer, who was now secured to the hoist, and it made it possible for the rescuer to get to the victim faster. It also allowed the helicopter's pilot to quickly recover the rescuer and the victim in the event of a mistake or accident.

Revised training methods were also put in place after the "Storm of the Century," one of the most intense nor'easters ever to strike the eastern United States. During the storm, which occurred in March of 1993, the entire eastern seaboard experienced extreme winds, freezing temperatures, and record snowfall. The Coast Guard, on high alert during the storm, responded to a number of distress calls, from Miami, Florida, to Cape Cod, Massachusetts. Coast Guard helicopters were used to operating in extreme conditions, with winds in excess of eighty knots and with seas up to 60 feet (about 18 m), and this storm was no different. But, while the Coast Guard made a number of successful rescues during the storm, there were several cases in which rescue swimmers deemed it too dangerous to enter the water.

After the storm, an inquiry was conducted to determine why the swimmers had declined to enter the water in conditions that were, in retrospect, perhaps not beyond their abilities. Many rescue swimmers admitted that in past situations they had felt pressured to deploy under conditions they felt were too difficult for them. Using this information, the Coast Guard later instituted a training program to expose rescue swimmers to more extreme rescue conditions. This advanced training improved the swimmers' ability to judge a rescue situation and helped them feel more confident in extreme situations.

In Training

3

In 1984, in response to the *Marine Electric* tragedy, a helicopter rescue swimmer program was established by the Coast Guard to expand marine rescue capabilities. It has since evolved from its original mission of open ocean rescue to what has now become the Coast Guard's extensive capability to assist people in distress in virtually any environment in which it operates.

Search-and-rescue swimmers must have the strength of a body builder and the swimming ability of a competitive Olympian. They must be able to pull drowning victims from stormy seas or raging rivers, all while keeping themselves safe and being aware of constantly changing conditions. Their strength, physical skills, and knowledge may make the difference between life and death—both for themselves and for those being rescued. Training to be a search-and-rescue swimmer is intensive and can take anywhere from five weeks, to acquire intermediate knowledge and skill, to more than two years, to learn to administer significant medical attention and conduct rescues in extreme conditions.

There are three training programs a candidate may consider when deciding to become a search-and-rescue swimmer. All of them require that a candidate be enlisted in the branch of the armed forces that offers the program. All of the candidates for these programs must already be in the military and must have completed boot camp and possibly other training programs. The U.S. Navy and the U.S. Marine Corps conduct a five-week program. Their rescue swimmers, sometimes referred to as SAR wet crewman, do most of their work from aircraft carriers. The U.S. Coast Guard offers an eighteen-week, highly intensive program. It trains its crews to conduct helicopter- and boat-based rescues where swimmers enter the water to assist victims in distress. And finally, the U.S. Air Force offers a very competitive and physically challenging program that graduates the most highly trained of rescuers. These PJs, or pararescue jumpers, are trained to perform not only sea-based but also land-based rescues.

U.S. Navy and Marine Corps

The U.S. Navy and Marine Corp's five-week Surface Rescue Swimmer Program begins with a one- to two-week course at the Swimmer Conditioning School, which serves to prepare candidates for the rigorous swimming and strength training required by the program. The conditioning school focuses on swimming techniques and physical fitness. After successfully completing the conditioning school, candidates continue on to the Surface Rescue Swimmer (SRS) School, a four-week program. Students in the SRS School become proficient with rescue equipment and learn basic first aid, CPR, resuscitation knowledge, and the skills necessary to recover and assist personnel during rescue operations. These operations could include the recovery of U.S. and foreign pilots, civilian or nonmilitary personnel, and even inanimate objects as necessary.

The U.S. Coast Guard Rescue Swimmer Training Program

The U.S. Coast Guard rescue swimmer training program has one of the highest student dropout rates of any special operations program in the military. Roughly seventy-five students go through the program each year, and fewer than half make it out. The Coast Guard's airborne rescue swimmers are trained at the Aviation Survival Technician/Rescue Swimmer School at Air Station Elizabeth City in North Carolina. The course is eighteen weeks long (more than three times the length of the U.S. Navy and Marine Corps schools), and the wait to enroll is long. Most often there is a two-year wait before a candidate can begin training in the program, and that's only if he or she passes a grueling physical fitness test that challenges even the most prepared athletes. Candidates must accomplish the following: forty-two push-ups in two minutes, fifty sit-ups in two minutes,

Students from the Aviation Rescue Swimmer School undergo rigorous and intensive training for search-and-rescue missions at sea. Here, they practice parachute disentanglement.

five pull-ups, a one-and-a-half-mile run in less than twelve minutes, and a five-hundred-yard swim in less than twelve minutes.

According to Coast Guard chief petty officer Thor Wentz, who helps run the school, many candidates give up before stepping foot in the pool. "As far as being difficult, it's extremely difficult," Wentz said. "We have an extremely high attrition rate, better than 50 percent. The not truly focused people will tend to disappear in the first couple of days."

Recently, the school disbanded an entire class within the first week of training, all because the physical demands proved too

Surface Rescue Swimmer Mission Statement

The mission of the naval surface rescue swimmer is to execute search-and-rescue operations from surface ships. Surface rescue swimmers are physically conditioned to routinely perform demanding rescues in hostile environments. Their expertise provides fleet commanders the ability to assist Department of Defense and civilian personnel in distress.

much for the candidates. "Twelve students showed up, and they were all gone within the first week," Wentz explained.

The curriculum begins with A-School, which includes instruction on rescue techniques, helicopter deployment techniques, and a variety of technical skills that range from small engine repair to parachute packing and maintenance. Successful completion of this course results in being awarded the aviation survival technician (AST) rating, the technical rating for a variety of aircraft and survival equipment maintenance.

After completion of A-School, all ASTs are sent to Petaluma, California, to attend the Coast Guard's Emergency Medical Technician (EMT) school. After three weeks of EMT training, all candidates must take and pass the National Registry of EMT's EMT-Basic test as part of their qualification to be a rescue swimmer.

Full qualification as a rescue swimmer can take up to a year from the first day of A-School. Once graduated, all rescue

Students at the Aviation Technical Training Center at Air Station Elizabeth City in North Carolina go through one of their vigorous daily workouts. Candidates for this program must pass a grueling physical fitness assessment.

swimmers must learn the aircraft systems and emergency procedures of their assigned aircraft.

U.S. Air Force Parajumpers

The most rigorous of all training programs is the U.S. Air Force parajumpers or pararescuemen (PJs) program. PJs are among the most highly trained emergency trauma specialists in the U.S. military. They must maintain an emergency medical technician-paramedic qualification throughout their careers. With this medical and rescue expertise, along with their deployment capabilities, PJs are able to perform life-saving missions in the world's most remote areas. The training program is highly specialized and includes intensive physical training. Only the best of the best complete this program. Nine out of every ten candidates drop out.

Training begins with the Pararescue Preparatory Course. This two-week course provides physical training under the guidance of sports physiologists and swimming trainers. It teaches the required skills to succeed in the Indoctrination Course that follows.

The Indoctrination Course is a ten-week course that recruits, selects, and trains PJs through extensive physical conditioning. Training includes physiological training, an obstacle course, marches, dive physics, dive tables, metric manipulations, medical terminology, CPR, weapons qualifications, PJ history, and a leadership reaction course. Candidates then enter U.S. Army Airborne School, where they learn basic parachuting skills—the skills necessary to drop into an area, including water or land, from an airplane. Then, candidates enter U.S. Air Force Combat Diver School. Trainees learn to use scuba and closed-circuit diving equipment and conduct underwater searches and basic recovery operations. The course provides training in water at depths of 130 feet (about 40 m) and stresses the development of underwater mobility under various conditions. Next, trainees complete U.S. Navy Underwater Egress Training, a course that teaches trainees how to get out of a sinking aircraft.

Trainees practice river survival at the U.S. Air Force Survival Training Center. The center also trains parajumpers, who are among the most highly trained emergency trauma specialists in the U.S. military.

The next step for trainees is to complete U.S. Air Force Basic Survival School. This two-and-a-half-week course teaches trainees to endure the harshest weather and environmental conditions. U.S. Army Military Free Fall Parachutist School is next. This course instructs trainees in freefall parachuting procedures. The five-week course provides wind tunnel training and in-air instruction focusing on stability, aerial maneuvers, air sense, and parachute opening procedures.

One skill set that distinguishes the PJs from other search-and-rescue swimmers is their emergency medical skills. All trainees complete the Paramedic Course, an intensive,

Stewart Smith

Stewart "Stew" Smith graduated from the U.S. Naval Academy in 1991. A former Navy SEAL, Smith trains young men and women for any profession that requires a physical fitness test—from law enforcement to military Special Forces. He has trained a number of men and women for the physical demands of being a search-and-rescue swimmer. Smith is the author of several fitness and self-defense books, including *The Complete Guide to Navy SEAL Fitness* and *Maximum Fitness*. As a military fitness trainer, Smith has also trained hundreds of students for the Navy SEALs, Special Forces, U.S. Air Force PJs, Ranger Training Brigade, and various law enforcement professions. His Web site, www.stewsmith.com, provides information on his books and includes customized personal training.

twenty-two-week course that teaches trainees how to manage trauma patients and provide emergency medical treatment immediately following a rescue. Upon graduation, an EMT-Paramedic certification is awarded through the National Registry of Emergency Medical Technicians, a national listing of all certified EMTs.

The final course is the Pararescue Recovery Specialist Course. This course qualifies trainees as pararescue recovery specialists. It prepares them for assignment to any pararescue unit world-wide. The twenty-four-week training includes field medical care and extrication basics, field tactics, mountaineering, combat tactics, advanced parachuting, and helicopter insertion/extraction.

PJs are trained as combatants and paramedics—operating on air, sea, and land—and are considered to be the air force equivalent to the elite Navy SEALs. During war they rescue downed pilots, special operations troops left behind, and other stranded military men and women. PJs are also active in peacetime, often retrieving NASA space equipment from bodies of water, but they also perform rescues in all types of natural disasters.

While there are three different programs to choose from, one group ensures that all search-and-rescue swimmer teams use the same techniques and observe the same policies. The Standardization Team, or "Stand" Unit, is made up of former rescue swimmers and observes all rescue swimmer units for consistency and conformity in training and rescue techniques. This enables any rescue team, anywhere, to work together if a large rescue mobilization is needed. In the case of Hurricane Katrina, when rescue crews from all over the United States and from many different organizations all came together, the groups could work with each other smoothly to save those in need.

"So Others May Live"

4

Adistress call is a call from a ship whose captain or crew has determined that they are in an emergency situation and need assistance. Any number of emergencies can result in a distress call: a fire on board, capsizing of the boat, or the vessel taking on water and beginning to sink. Sometimes even a severe injury can result in a distress call.

Once a distress call is made, the search-and-rescue team will need particular information to know what type of situation they are dealing with and what type of assistance the vessel needs. They will often ask the "Three Ps."

The "Three Ps"

The Coast Guard has three basic questions it will ask to make its initial assessment of the rescue situation. These basic questions cover the Three Ps: position, problem, and people. First, the Coast Guard will want to know the position or location of the ship that is in trouble. If for some reason the ship and its crew

Radarman 1st Class Travis Costigan monitors vessels entering Puget Sound in Washington State. Costigan tracks the movement of vessels and responds to distress calls when a vessel becomes endangered.

lose contact with the Coast Guard, knowing the position of the ship will enable the Coast Guard to at least send a rescue team in response. Second, it will want to know what the problem is. Is the boat taking on water? Is there a fire on board? Is there a medical emergency? This information will let the Coast Guard know what type of resources it will need for the rescue. Third, it will want to know about the people on board. How many are there? Are they military personnel or civilians? Are there children and women? With the basic information from the Three Ps, the Coast Guard is best prepared to assist in a situation.

Once the basic information is obtained, the next series of questions the Coast Guard asks is referred to as amplifying information. This may include a description of the boat, if there are any medical emergencies on board, what the on-scene weather is, and if there are any emergency supplies on board (e.g., life rafts, flares, life jackets, food and water, etc.). Sometimes the amplifying information can change the way the Coast Guard approaches the search-and-rescue operation. For example, if the weather is calm, with little wind, and the vessel is not too far offshore, the Coast Guard may send a smaller rescue vessel. If the weather is bad and there are severe injuries, the Coast Guard may send a helicopter, sometimes called a helo, or a larger cutter. When a search-and-rescue swimmer has to get into the water to get people out of a life raft, the more knowledge the rescue swimmer has, the more prepared the rescuer will be.

Search-and-Rescue Emergency Phases

The Coast Guard has three emergency phases that determine each situation when a distress call is made. The Coast Guard will determine which phase it is in based on the information given to it during the call. The better the information, the more accurately it can decide how best to perform the rescue. The Uncertainty Phase is the phase in which there is a situation that needs to be monitored but does not require deploying a rescue crew. For example, the Coast Guard might receive a call from a fisherman's wife saying that her husband should have been back to the dock three hours ago. The Coast Guard will begin trying to contact the vessel and the local marinas, other vessels in the area, or other agencies that may have knowledge of the location of the missing ship.

The Alert Phase is when an aircraft, ship, other craft, or person on board a vessel is having difficulty and may need assistance but is not in immediate danger. To use the example of the wife again, in this phase she might call back to say that her husband has a heart condition and he forgot his medication. At this point a search-and-rescue unit may be launched to search the area of the last known position of the boat.

The third phase is the Distress Phase. This is the phase when there is a reasonable certainty that an aircraft, a ship, or the people on board are in danger and require immediate assistance. The situation with the husband needing heart medication would be upgraded to the distress phase if night fell or the weather grew more severe. In this phase, the Coast Guard launches a rescue vessel immediately.

Entering a Dangerous Rescue Situation

After the distress call is received and the situation is evaluated, the search-and-rescue team must be deployed. Many times, the situation is a dangerous one that requires the search-and-rescue swimmer to work with his or her team to decide how best to approach. The search-and-rescue swimmer must have a number

Aviation survival technicians train in a number of scenarios and rescue techniques. The more highly skilled a rescue swimmer, the more challenging the situations he or she can successfully face.

of survival skills in order to maintain his or her safety while tending to the situation. Swimmers must have flexibility, strength, and endurance, and they must be able to function for thirty minutes in heavy seas. They also must learn eight different water deployment procedures; eleven ways to approach, carry, and release a survivor; seven ways to release various types of equipment if the victim is in the military; and several ways to detangle different parachutes and backpacks. Additionally, they may be required to provide basic prehospital life support for injured survivors. These are among the most basic of skills a rescue swimmer needs to know.

A Team Effort

A search-and-rescue swimmer and crew work as a team to conduct a rescue on the high seas. Each person on the team has responsibilities that help the rescue go smoothly and make it a success. A team, at its most basic, is made up of the search-and-rescue swimmer, the pilot or pilots that fly the helicopter, and a flight mechanic. The search-and-rescue swimmer is responsible for entering the water, assisting the victims in getting into the rescue basket, and getting them safely into the helicopter. The search-and-rescue swimmer communicates the situation to crewmates using hand signals to indicate where the pilots and flight mechanics should position the helicopter. Depending on his or her level of training, the search-and-rescue swimmer may also provide medical treatment to the victims.

Cold-Water Survival Do's and Don'ts

Maintaining body temperature is crucial to cold-water survival. Even good swimmers drown due to the strains of swimming in cold water.

Do:

- Get out of the water as soon as possible if you are near a boat or the shore.
- Huddle together or in a group facing each other to maintain body heat.
- Stay with the boat. The chances of survival, and of being found, increase if you stay with the boat.

Don't:

- Panic.
- Remove clothing, even if it's heavy clothing. Clothing can help trap air that can keep you warm.
- Swim unless you can reach a nearby boat, fellow survivor, or floating object. Swimming in cold water can lower body temperature thirty-two times faster than cold air.

An MH-60S Knighthawk helicopter recovers a search-and-rescue swimmer in the Atlantic Ocean. The swimmer was conducting a training mission in preparation for his certification test.

The helicopter is usually flown by two pilots. Pilots prepare and study flight plans, precheck and monitor weather conditions, control the helicopter on the ground and in the air, study information from flight instruments, check equipment, and maintain the condition of the helicopter prior to and after rescue missions. The pilots have extensive training in maritime navigation and can arrive at a location using only the coordinates provided by the distress call. They must position the helicopter directly above the victim or victims, communicate to the air station the status of the situation, and call for additional assistance if necessary.

The rescue swimmer can enter the water either by diving from the helicopter or by being lowered into the water by a flight mechanic using a hoist. The wire hoist can lift 600 pounds (272 kilograms) from 200 feet (61 m) below the helicopter. Sometimes the hoist has a rescue basket attached. The basket can fit a person inside of it and can be reeled up into the helicopter to get the victim inside the aircraft. When the rescue swimmer is ready for the rescue basket, the flight mechanic lowers the basket to the swimmer using a handheld control. This job takes concentration and precision under sometimes extreme conditions.

Rescues That Made History

Search-and-rescue swimmers have been involved in a number of rescues that have made history. Many rescuers have been awarded honors by the armed forces for their bravery and courage under extreme conditions. Here are just a few of their stories.

Distinguished Flying Cross Award

On December 10, 1987, Air Station Sitka, in Alaska, received a distress call from a fishing vessel that was taking on water about ten miles (sixteen kilometers) southwest of Sitka, a seaside community in southeastern Alaska. A helicopter was quickly launched to search for the vessel, but the weather conditions were terrible. A severe snowstorm kept visibility to less than a quarter mile. The seas were also extremely high, with 25- to 30-foot waves (7.6 to 9.1 m), and the wind was blowing at thirty-five knots with gusts up to seventy knots. Aboard the

The Distinguished Flying Cross Award recognizes single acts of heroism or extraordinary achievement. The U.S. Congress established the award on July 2, 1926.

fishing vessel was a thirty-three-year-old man and his six-year-old son, both of whom were wearing survival suits.

Despite numerous attempts, the pilot and hoist operator were unable to get the rescue basket to the man and son. The pilot convinced the father that the only chance for a rescue was to enter the water with his son, where they could then get into the rescue basket. With the son strapped to his chest, the father jumped over the side and into the water. The man's survival suit immediately began to leak and fill with water. The man and his son attempted to get into the basket several times, but they could not. The pilot turned to Jeffery Tunks, a rescue swimmer, and directed him to prepare for deployment. In seconds, Tunks was in the turbulent water and swimming to assist the man and his son. Fighting heavy seas and winds, Tunks struggled but succeeded in getting the two into the rescue basket, where they were hoisted into the helicopter.

Meanwhile, as Tunks was trying to get back into the aircraft, the helicopter was fighting extremely gusty winds. As he fought, he was dragged through an enormous sea swell, or wave. He

The members of the Coast Guard crew that saved the passengers of the *Mary Lynn* receive Distinguished Flying Cross awards.

lost his mask and snorkel and sustained a minor back injury but was recovered; and with the two survivors safely aboard, the helicopter returned to Sitka. For his courage, and for deploying into dangerous conditions that had not been previously faced by other rescue swimmers, Tunks became the first rescue swimmer to earn the Distinguished Flying Cross Award.

The Distinguished Flying Cross was established by an act of Congress on July 2, 1926. It is awarded to any person who, "while serving in any capacity with the Armed Forces, distinguished himself or herself by heroism or extraordinary achievement while participating in aerial flight. The performance of the act of heroism must be evidenced by voluntary action above and beyond the call of duty." Furthermore, the achievement must be so exceptional as to clearly set the individual apart from his or her peers or from others in similar circumstances. Awards are made only to recognize single acts of heroism or extraordinary achievement and are not made in recognition of sustained operational activities against an armed enemy.

Air Medal Awarded to First Female Rescue Swimmer

Since the inception of the Coast Guard Rescue Swimmer Program, only six women have served as Coast Guard rescue swimmers. There were many protests at the thought of having women enrolled in the program. The male-dominated Coast Guard questioned whether women would have the physical ability to complete the training. One woman who proved them wrong was Kelly Mogk.

On May 23, 1986, Mogk became the first female to graduate from Navy Rescue Swimmer School. Prior to Mogk's enrollment, only one other woman had earned admission to the navy's program, but she had resigned before completing the program. Mogk believed passing was within her reach, despite the fact that she felt her instructors wanted her to quit.

"They were doing everything in their power to make me quit," Mogk said in an interview with Martha LaGuardia-Kotite for the book *So Others May Live*. "Once they realized I would not give up and was doing well, it became less and less a big deal to them. It was tough, a tough school for everybody. A lot of people failed."

Mogk wanted to work in aviation and be on the front lines of rescue missions. This ambition—and the desire to defy her instructors—was what kept her going during the difficult training program. "What gave me my determination was when the instructors were telling me, 'You're going to fail; I'll give you two weeks.' So there was a little bit of 'I'm going to prove them wrong,'" said Mogk.

After successfully completing her training, Mogk graduated from the Coast Guard program and became the first woman to qualify as a rescue swimmer in not only the Coast Guard, but

Stephanie Kelley, winner of a Yahoo! Fantasy Careers contest, is given the opportunity to train with search-and-rescue swimmers at Air Station Houston. To this day, few women become search-and-rescue swimmers.

in all of the military services. But Mogk's real test of strength would happen on January 3, 1989, when the pilot and weapons officer of an Oregon National Guard F-4 fighter jet bailed out 35 miles (56 km) west of Tillamook Bay, Oregon.

The Coast Guard responded to the distress call by dispatching a helicopter from Air Station Astoria, piloted by Lieutenant Commander Bill Peterson and Lieutenant Junior Grade Bill Harper. Also aboard were Petty Officer Reese, a flight mechanic, and Mogk. The rescue crew arrived to horrendous conditions. There were 100-foot (30.5 m) ceilings (overhanging clouds), a scant quarter mile (.4 km) of visibility, and 20-foot (6 m) seas. It was mid-winter, and the temperatures were below freezing. After a search of the area, the pilots finally located two rafts but could find only one of the pilots. The helicopter approached the raft and hovered overhead as the crew evaluated the situation. With the go-ahead from the pilots, Mogk jumped from the helicopter into the freezing waters below. She swam to the pilot and realized that he was tangled in his parachute. After evaluating the pilot, Mogk also concluded that he had several broken bones and was suffering from hypothermia. He was having considerable trouble keeping his head above water. Mogk began to work on untangling the pilot from his parachute. She was finally able to cut the pilot free and help him into a rescue basket so that Peterson and Harper could hoist him into the helicopter.

Mogk was now suffering from severe hypothermia. Her dry suit had leaked, allowing the frigid water in, and her fingers and hands were numb. As she was looking unsuccessfully for the second pilot, a second search-and-rescue team arrived, allowing Mogk to return to the helicopter and to Air Station Astoria. After an extensive search, the second rescue team located the pilot, who unfortunately had gotten tangled in his parachute, was caught under the raft, and drowned. For her exceptional skill and determined effort during the rescue, Mogk was awarded the prestigious Air Medal.

The Air Medal is awarded to any person who has distinguished him- or herself by meritorious achievement while participating in aerial flight. Awards may be made to recognize single acts of merit or heroism. Mogk become the first female rescue swimmer to receive an award for heroism.

The Coast Guard Medal

On April 1, 1991, Air Station San Francisco received a distress call that two boys were trapped inside a coastal cave. A helicopter with a rescue swimmer was deployed to rescue the boys. Arriving on the scene, the team realized that the boys could not be recovered directly by the helicopter. The boys were located deep inside a cave and could only be reached by a rescue swimmer. With the helicopter hovering at the mouth of the cave, Petty Officer Steve Frye jumped from the aircraft into the water and then swam into the cave. He found the boys hanging on a ledge that was about to be submerged by the rising tide. Frye's only option was to take one boy at a time and swim out of the

To keep current on their qualifications and certifications, search-and-rescue swimmers must continually train and hone their skills. Here, a search-and-rescue swimmer simulates a rescue mission.

cave. The strong tide repeatedly pushed him back into the cave and against the rocks. After several attempts, Frye was finally able to get out of the cave with the first boy. Even though he was extremely tired from fighting the tidewaters, Frye reentered the cave for the second boy. Again he battled the heavy tide and waves, working hard to protect both himself and the boy from crashing into the rocks. Frye eventually made it out with the second boy. The two boys and Frye were hoisted aboard the aircraft and transported to a hospital for evaluation. Other than exhaustion and a broken finger, Frye was in good condition. For his extraordinary heroism, Frye received the Coast Guard Medal, which is awarded to any member of the armed forces who performs an act of heroism that does not involve conflict with an enemy.

Glossary

air station A base for military aircraft.

bow The front of a boat.

capsize When a boat or ship is tipped over until it is upside down.

ceiling The height of the lowest layer of clouds.

closed-circuit diving equipment Scuba equipment in which the air breathed in from the scuba tank is processed to make it fit to breathe again.

cutter Any Coast Guard vessel that measures 65 feet (about 20 m) or more in length and has living accommodations for its crew.

eastern seaboard Also called Atlantic seaboard; the eastern-most coastal states in the United States, which touch the Atlantic Ocean and stretch up to Canada.

hypothermia A condition in which an organism's temperature drops below that required for normal metabolism and bodily functions.

knot A measurement of speed for a maritime vessel.

levee An artificial slope or wall created to minimize flooding.

mountaineering The sport of walking, hiking, trekking, and climbing up mountains.

Navy SEALs An elite special force of the U.S. Navy that is used in unconventional warfare, guerrilla warfare, foreign internal defense, direct action, counterterrorism, specific enemy snatch and grab, specific enemy assassination, hostage rescue, and special reconnaissance operations.

reservist A person who is a member of a reserve military force; reservists are otherwise civilians, and in peacetime have careers outside the military. Reservists usually go for training on an annual basis to refresh their skills.

scuba Acronym for self-contained underwater breathing apparatus; scuba gear is the equipment necessary to breathe underwater during scuba diving.

sports physiology The study of the psychological and mental factors that influence, or are influenced by, the participation and performance in sport, exercise, and physical activity.

visibility The measure of distance at which an object or light can be clearly identified.

For More Information

National Registry of Emergency Medical Technicians
Rocco V. Morando Building
6610 Busch Boulevard
P.O. Box 29233
Columbus, OH 43229
(614) 888-4484
Web site: http://www.nremt.org
The organization established and implemented uniform
   requirements for the certification and recertification of
   emergency medical technicians. It also maintains a registry
   of all those who have been certified as emergency medical
   technicians.

United States Coast Guard Academy
Admissions
31 Mohegan Avenue
New London, CT 06320
(800) 883-8724

Web site: http://www.uscga.edu

The United States Coast Guard Academy is a U.S. military academy that provides education to future officers of the United States Coast Guard.

United States Naval Academy

121 Blake Road

Annapolis, MD 21402

Web site: http://www.usna.edu

The Naval Academy, founded in 1845, gives young men and women the up-to-date academic and professional training needed to be effective naval and marine officers in their assignments after graduation.

Web Sites

Due to the changing nature of Internet links, Rosen Publishing has developed an online list of Web sites related to the subject of this book. This site is updated regularly. Please use this link to access the list:

http://www.rosenlinks.com/exc/sere

For Further Reading

Drury, Bob. *The Rescue Season: The Heroic Story of Parajumpers on the Edge of the World.* New York, NY: Simon & Schuster, 2001.

Hoover, Gerald R. *Brotherhood of the Fin: A Coast Guard Rescue Swimmer's Story.* Tucson, AZ: Wheatmark, 2007.

LaGuardia-Kotite, Martha J. *So Others May Live: Coast Guard's Rescue Swimmers: Saving Lives, Defying Death.* Guilford, CT: The Lyons Press, 2006.

Lewan, Todd. *The Last Run: A True Story of Rescue and Redemption on the Alaska Seas.* New York, NY: Harper Paperbacks, 2005.

Moyer, Susan M. *Hurricane Katrina: Stories of Rescue, Recovery and Rebuilding in the Eye of the Storm.* Champaign, IL: Spotlight Press LLC, 2005.

Nelson, Pete, and Jack Brehm. *That Others May Live: The True Story of a PJ, a Member of America's Most Daring Rescue Force.* New York, NY: Crown, 2000.

Walker, Spike. *Coming Back Alive: The True Story of the Most Harrowing Search-and-rescue Mission Ever Attempted on Alaska's High Seas.* New York, NY: St. Martin's Griffin, 2002.

Bibliography

Coast Guard Aviation History. "A History of Coast Guard Aviation." Retrieved October 30, 2007 (http://uscgaviationhistory.aoptero.org/history04.html).

HSC-3 Merlins. "Surface Rescue Swimmer Mission Statement." Retrieved November, 2, 2007 (http://www.hsc3.navy.mil/sarmm/SARMM%20WEB/links/Fitness%20CD/SRSP.htm).

Krueger, Curtis. "Coast Guard Rescue Crew Braves Katrina's Winds." *St Petersburg Times*, August 30, 2005. Retrieved November 3, 2007 (http://www.sptimes.com/2005/08/30/Tampabay/Coast_Guard_rescue_cr.shtml).

LaGuardia-Kotite, Martha. "Pioneers in Aviation." Coast Guard Channel. Retrieved November 2, 2007 (http://www.coastguardchannel.com/images/spclFeatures/AuthorsCorner/Pioneers_in_Aviation.pdf).

Markley, David. "The World's Elite Search-and-rescue Operatives." *Air Beat*. Retrieved October 13, 2007 (http://www.alea.org/public/airbeat/back_issues/may_jun_2005/sar2.htm).

Military.com "Helicopter Rescue Swimmers—Saving Lives Every Day." Retrieved September 19, 2007 (http://www.military.com/NewContent/0,13190,Smith_091405,00.html).

Military Sealift Command. "Surface Rescue Swimmer Development Program." Retrieved November 2, 2007 (http://www.msc.navy.mil/civmar/training/trainingbulletin02-05.htm).

Philadelphia Inquirer. "The Wreck of the Marine Electric." Retrieved October 29, 2007 (http://www.rpcontent.com/wreck_of_the_marine_electric.htm).

Ryan, Doris. "Navy Medicine Researcher Helps SAR Swimmers Get & Stay Fit." U.S. Navy. Retrieved October 29, 2007 (http://www.navy.mil/search/display.asp?story_id=3660).

Sailonline.com "Handling Distress and Help Calls." Retrieved November 1, 2007 (http://www.sailonline.com/seamanship/coastie/distress.html).

Sample, Doug. "Coast Guard Rescue Swimmer Training." American Forces Press Service. Retrieved October 22, 2007 (http://usmilitary.about.com/od/coastguard/a/cgrescueswimmer.htm).

Sample, Doug. "Coast Guard School Tough Swimming, Few Pass Rescue Course." U.S. Department of Defense. Retrieved November 13, 2007 (http://www.defenselink.mil/news/newsarticle.aspx?id=25362).

Seafarers International Union. "*Marine Electric* Sinking in 1983 Sparked Safety Reforms." Retrieved October 13, 2007 (http://www.seafarers.org/log/2003/022003/marineelectric.xml).

U. S. Coast Guard. "Coast Guard Response to Hurricane Katrina." Retrieved November 1, 2007 (http://www.uscg.mil/hq/g-cp/comrel/factfile/Factcards/Hurricane_Katrina.htm).

U.S. Coast Guard. "U.S. Coast Guard Rescue Swimmers Exceed 4,000 Lives Saved." Published January 23, 2001. Retrieved October 15, 2007 (http://www.uscg.mil/d7/units/as-savannah/pao/ast-pao.htm).

Index

About the Author

Laura La Bella is a writer and editor. She lives and works in Rochester, N.Y., with her husband, Matthew, a social studies teacher. While in college, La Bella was a lifeguard on an air force base. As part of her training, she completed exercises and rescue drills with air force pilots. She also served as a swimming instructor.

Photo Credits

Cover, pp. 1, 4, 6 ,11, 20–21, 24, 29, 34, 38, 43, 45, 53, 55, 57, 59, 62 U.S. Coast Guard; pp. 7, 9, 15, 44 © AP Photos; p. 19 © Corbis Sygma; pp. 31, 35 © Getty Images; pp. 27, 41, 55 U.S. Navy.

Designer: Les Kanturek; **Editor:** Peter Herman
Photo Researcher: Marty Levick